SHOVEL KNIGHT

Codes
of
Shovelry
HANDBOOK

GROSSET & DUNLAP
Penguin Young Readers Group
An Imprint of Penguin Random House LLC

YACHT CLUB
GAMES

Shovel Knight is a trademark of Yacht Club Games.
© 2017 Yacht Club Games L.L.C. All rights reserved. Published by Grosset & Dunlap, an imprint of Penguin Random House LLC, 345 Hudson Street, New York, New York 10014. GROSSET & DUNLAP is a trademark of Penguin Random House LLC.
Manufactured in China.

ISBN 9781101996027   10 9 8 7 6 5 4 3 2 1

SHOVEL KNIGHT

Codes
of
Shovelry
HANDBOOK

by Kevin Panetta

Grosset & Dunlap
An Imprint of Penguin Random House

Table of Contents

THE CODE OF SHOVELRY

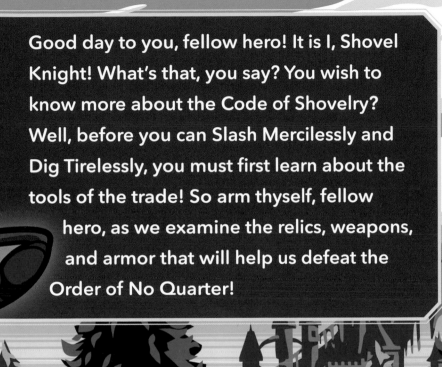

Good day to you, fellow hero! It is I, Shovel Knight! What's that, you say? You wish to know more about the Code of Shovelry? Well, before you can Slash Mercilessly and Dig Tirelessly, you must first learn about the tools of the trade! So arm thyself, fellow hero, as we examine the relics, weapons, and armor that will help us defeat the Order of No Quarter!

Shovel Knight's Motto:
Slash Mercilessly! Dig Tirelessly!

RELICS

Meet Chester

Hey there! Did the blue guy send you? Well, if you're searchin' for relics, you've come to the right place! Ol' Chester has exactly what you're lookin' for, as long as you've got some dough. Wait . . . you don't wanna buy nothin'? Well, I guess I could just tell ya what all these things do. Maybe you'll find somethin' ya like and that'll change your mind!

WHAT ARE RELICS?

What are relics? Who's askin'?! Oh, it's you! Well, let me tell ya, then. Relics are tools a traveler can buy throughout the world. Besides your Shovel Blade, relics are the most useful tools you can have, and I'm happy to sell them to a wealthy traveler like yourself.

WHERE TO FIND RELICS

Sometimes ya can find relics
in secret places while you're
out fightin' bad guys, but
even if you miss the locations,
you can always buy 'em from
your pal Chester (that's me!)
in the Village!

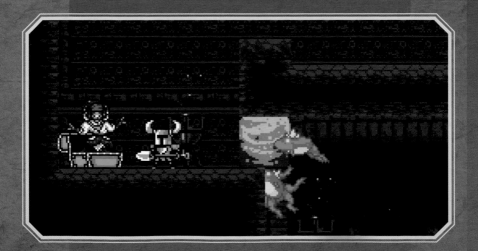

FISHING ROD

Name: Fishing Rod

Description: Cast into a pit and wait for a bite! Keep an eye out for sparkly fishing spots!

Location: Village

Price: 1,250 (Village)

Magic Casting Cost: 6

Damage Points: 1

Tips and Tricks: Try fishing flying sacks that are below you for a nice surprise. Use with a Troupple Chalice, page 26.

Give a knight a fish and he'll eat for a day. Give a knight a Fishing Rod and he'll be snaggin' Troupples for the rest of his life!

Useful for catchin' fish and food (and sometimes even for whackin' an enemy on the head), the Fishing Rod is one of the first relics that Shovel Knight gets his blue-armored hands on, and it's also one of the most useful!

Ye Olde Relic Facts

- ❖ Buy the Fishing Rod from Chester in the Village.

- ❖ Use the Fishing Rod whenever you see a sparkling pit.

- ❖ Besides fish and food, the Fishing Rod can also catch treasure and sometimes even music sheets!

Percent Chance of Fishing Up:

Small Fish	37%
Medium Fish	27%
Large Fish	9%
Sword	9%
Apple Core	9%
Skull	9%
Lava Fish	100% (in lava)

Other Items to Fish

Goldfish	You can't eat it, but these golden gills will net you 350 gold!
Music Sheet	Return these sheets to the Bard for 500 gold per sheet!
Ichor of Renewal	Refills all health and magic. Popular with adventurers!
Ichor of Boldness	Become invincible for ten seconds. Great for those tough spots!
Ichor of Fortune	Absorb nearby treasure for sixty seconds . . . even through walls!

CHAOS SPHERE

Name: Chaos Sphere

Description: An orb of boundless combat potential. Give it a good throw!

Location: Village

Price: 2,500 (Village)

Magic Casting Cost: 6

Damage Points: 1

Tips and Tricks: This bad boy relic will cut right through a Boss's Health! Adventurers can have two Chaos Spheres out at one time.

A bouncin' sphere of, well, chaos, the Chaos Sphere causes destruction wherever it's thrown! Sure, it looks like a bouncy ball, but that don't stop it from takin' out a swarm of Propeller Rats with one mighty toss!

Ye Olde Relic Facts

- ❖ Buy the Chaos Sphere from Chester in the Village.
- ❖ It's green, it's mean, and it'll clean the screen of fiends.
- ❖ Defeat five enemies within five seconds with the Chaos Sphere to get the Super Sphere feat!

Greetings, traveler! I'm not sure we've met before. My name is the Bard! I'm sure you are very weary from your journey. Well, nothing lifts the spirits quite like a song! So sit back, relax, and listen to:

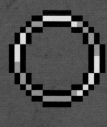

The Hoop Kid

Hoop Kid, Hoop Kid playing games
Oh, that Hoop Jump I must tame.
Bouncing, flying through the air,
"Hooper," call me, if you dare.
Hoop Kid, Hoop Kid playing games
Oh, that Hoop Jump I must tame.

Along the way, you will encounter many friends and foes. Most importantly, you will learn the significance of your quest to the people of The Valley.

The Ballad of the Hedge Farmer

There was a farmer we all know, the prickliest of all.

Who would see things with his two eyes, and wonder what he saw.

He met a man, a burrower blue, with shovel in his hand.

A hero known across the land!

The man said, "I am Shovel Knight"; the farmer said he lied.

The farmer asked for proof and the trowel-clad knight decried:

"I'll dig this dirt and then you'll see that I am who I claim!"

He dug and the Hedge Farmer exclaimed:

"You really are the Shovel Knight, our land will now be saved!

We've been in darkness many years. You're back. We say, HOORAY!

I wish you well upon your quest to save us from this plight!

You are a great hero, Shovel Knight!"

FLARE WAND

Name: Flare Wand

Description: It's a wand that shoots fireballs! Watch your magic meter!

Location: Pridemoor Keep

Price: ◊ 1,000 (Field); ◊ 2,000 (Village)

Magic Casting Cost: 4

Damage Points: 1

Tips and Tricks: Adventurers can have two fireballs on-screen at one time.

Conjure Fiery Blasts!

What could be better than a wand that shoots fire?! The Flare Wand is great for takin' out bad guys who you don't want to get too close to you, so go ahead and attack enemies from far away and show 'em who's boss!

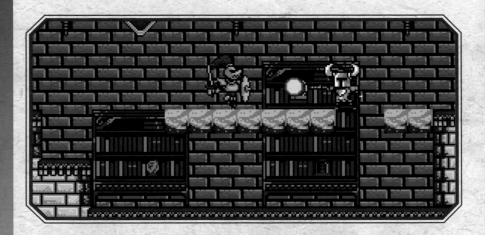

Ye Olde Relic Facts

- ❖ Defeat an enemy from all the way across the screen to earn the Flare Wander feat.

- ❖ Find the Flare Wand in a secret room in King Knight's castle, Pridemoor Keep!

Meet the Magicist

Oh, hello. I can increase your magic, good? You use magic when you use relics, yes? I can help you increase your maximum magic, yes?

Magic Upgrades

Magic Upgrade Cost		
Max MP	40	🔷1,500
Max MP	50	🔷2,200
Max MP	60	🔷2,800
Max MP	70	🔷3,400
Max MP	80	🔷4,000
Max MP	90	🔷6,000
Max MP	100	🔷8,000

PHASE LOCKET

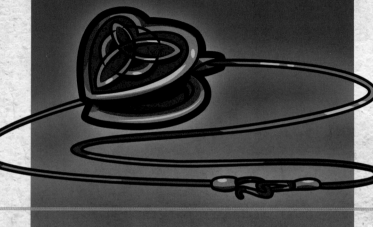

Name: Phase Locket

Description: Escape from all harm . . . briefly. You can even walk on spikes!

Location: The Lich Yard

Price: 1,000 (Field); 2,000 (Village)

Magic Casting Cost: 8

Damage Points: N/A

Tips and Tricks: When activated, this relic protects you from harm for three seconds. Land and run on spikes without dying!

Have ya ever wanted to be invincible? The Phase Locket lets you turn invincible for three seconds at a time and avoid all damage, even from spikes!

Ye Olde Relic Facts

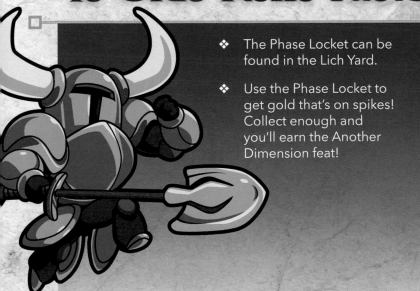

❖ The Phase Locket can be found in the Lich Yard.

❖ Use the Phase Locket to get gold that's on spikes! Collect enough and you'll earn the Another Dimension feat!

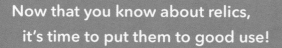

Now that you know about relics,
it's time to put them to good use!

FOREST OF PHASING

The first of three Relic Courses.
You can make it through the Forest
of Phasing only by using the Phase
Locket relic!

Croaker Puns

Welcome to Showtime at the Village Juice Bar! I'm Croaker and I'm toad-ally excited to be your host! Excuse my voice, though—I know it sounds a bit froggy! Anyway, on with the show! This ought to be a real ribbit-ing presentation.

Did you hear about the unlucky fisherman on a rainy day? It was a reel problem.

The Hedge Farmer ate everybody else's food at breakfast. What a hog.

❖ There is a feat for listening to all of Croaker's puns. See if you can listen to them all without croaking.

TROUPPLE CHALICE

Name: Troupple Chalice

Damage Points: N/A

Description: There are two Troupple Chalices. They are both vessels for storing mythical ichor.

Location: Village

Price: 1,500 (Village)

Magic Casting Cost: N/A

Tips and Tricks: Make sure to visit the Troupple King to have him fill the chalice with ichor. To the right is a full list of ichors. Best used with the Fishing Rod.

Hello, fish friend! All hail the Troupple King! If you seek knowledge of all things Troupple, you've swum to the right lake . . . erm . . . place! The Troupple Chalice is a cup, of that I am shore, but this is no ordinary dinnerware. No! This chalice holds a mystical liquid known as ichor that can either restore health, make you invincible, or help you gather treasure!

A Vessel for Storing Mystical Ichor

Ichor Name	Description	Tips for Use/Places to Use
Ichor of Renewal	Refills all health and magic. Popular with adventurers!	❖ You can carry two Ichors of Renewal into every stage. ❖ If you're having trouble with a boss, an Ichor of Renewal can help take the edge off the fight. ❖ Make sure to hold off on using an Ichor of Renewal near pits and spikes. Once it's used in a stage, you'll have to visit the Trouple King to get a refill. ❖ Make sure to carry an Ichor of Renewal with you when taking on the Order of No Quarter Roundtable Battle!
Ichor of Boldness	Become invincible for ten seconds. Great for those tough spots!	❖ Having trouble with some pesky spikes? Unable to get past some baddies hassling you? Down this ichor and run right through all your problems! WARNING: Death pits will still be an issue for adventurers.
Ichor of Fortune	Absorb nearby treasure for sixty seconds . . . even through walls!	❖ Are you trying to collect hard-to-reach flying sacks of money? This ichor is for you!

Ye Olde Relic Facts

❖ There are three types of ichor.

❖ You know who the Trouple King is, don't you?

You don't?! Well, turn the page and find out!

THE TROUPPLE KING

Hey, fish friend! All hail the Troupple King! King of fruit and fish, long may his stem grow!

Ye Olde Troupple King Fish Facts

- ❖ Lives in Troupple Pond.

- ❖ Leader of the Troupples.

- ❖ Is a really great dancer. Seriously. This mackerel has got some moves!

- ❖ Gets mad if anyone soils his waters.

- ❖ Can provide ichor to replenish life, capture treasure, and provide invincibility.

DUST KNUCKLES

Name: Dust Knuckles

Description: Dash through dirt and foes alike! Propels with each punch!

Location: Lost City

Price: 3,000 (Field); 3,500 (Village)

Magic Casting Cost: 2

Damage Points: 1

Tips and Tricks: Use the knuckles to cut through enemies that take a ton of hits.

Punch through dirt with the greatest of ease with the best knuckles this side of the Lost City! I'll make you a deal, too! If you can find ol' Chester in the Lost City, I'll sell ya these mighty mittens for 3,000 gold! That's a 500-gold discount!

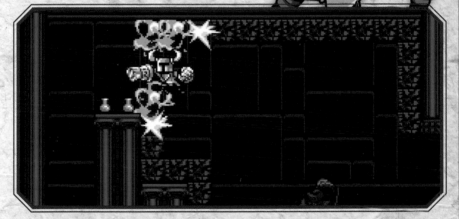

Ye Olde Relic Facts

- ❖ The gold Dust Knuckles really bring out the blue in your armor.

- ❖ Great for punching stuff, especially when trying to get gold hidden behind blocks.

- ❖ Stay in the air for more than four seconds with the Dust Knuckles to earn the Knuckle Down feat!

KNUCKLER'S QUARRY

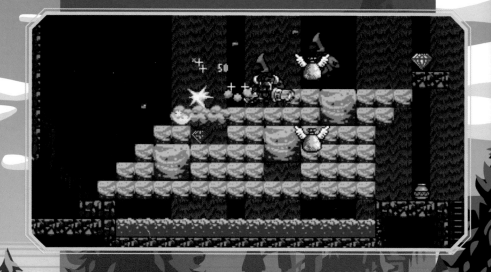

The second of three Relic Courses.
You can only make it through
Knuckler's Quarry by using the
Dust Knuckles relic!

Cooking with the Gastronomer

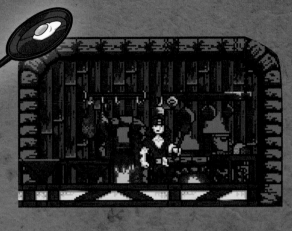

Food	Region
Dozedrake Steak	Plains
Royal Feast	Pridemoor Keep
Stewed Tadvolt Legs	The Lich Yard
Moler Crown Roast	Lost City
Fairy Fricassee	Explodatorium
Ratsploder Surprise	Explodatorium
Teethalon Nigiri	Iron Whale
Peanut Butter and Floatsome Sandwich	Flying Machine
Chilled Spinwulf	Stranded Ship
Blackened Black Griffoth's Tail	Tower of Fate
Braised Divedrake's Tail	Plains
Ichor-Infused Onigiri	Special Import to the Village

THROWING ANCHOR

Name: Throwing Anchor

Description: An unstoppable arc of destruction. Crush foes above and below!

Location: Iron Whale

Price: 3,000 (Field); 3,500 (Village)

Magic Casting Cost: 6

Damage Points: 1

Tips and Tricks: The Throwing Anchor is super effective against Propeller Knight while he flies around his ship.

Eels alive! This relic was tough to come by, let me tell ya! Don't believe me? Why don't you try being stuck on the end of a Teethalon's head for a while! Anyway, the Throwing Anchor is a big ol' heavy thing that you can toss in the air to take out enemies! It's pretty cool, in a nautical kinda way!

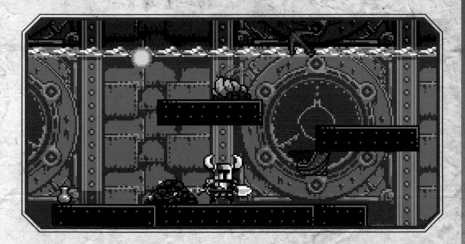

Ye Olde Relic Facts

- ❖ The Throwing Anchor is the heaviest of all the relics.

- ❖ Defeat three enemies with one throw to earn the Arc of Iron feat!

ALCHEMY COIN

Name: Alchemy Coin

Description: Toss a coin for a chance at riches. If you're lucky, you can win big!

Location: Explodatorium

Price: 🪙3,000 (Field); 🪙3,500 (Village)

Magic Casting Cost: 8

Damage Points: 2

Tips and Tricks: To hit multiple enemies, try swinging your Shovel Blade at the coin as it bounces back to you to start up a volley.

Toss a Coin for a Chance at Riches

Alchemy Coin Drops	% Chance of What Enemies Will Drop
Diamonds (+100 gold)	10%
Gold (+60 gold)	40%
Silver (+4 gold)	50%

You're not gonna *believe* what I just found in this chest. Want to see? It's an Alchemy Coin! It turns small enemies into gold! Because, let's be honest . . . what would ya rather have? A Blorb or some gold?! (It's some gold, right? Although, I guess a pet Blorb might be pretty cool, too.)

Ye Olde Relic Facts

- ❖ You can hit the Alchemy Coin with your shovel to start a volley . . .

- ❖ . . . and if you whack the same coin five times, you can earn the Reflected Riches feat!

Greetings again, traveler! We've of course met before, but in case you've forgotten, I am the Bard! Anyway, I hope my last tune didn't leave you on a sour note, because I've got another ditty for you! This one is called:

The Water-Carrying Lass

A girl who is quite pretty,
and always walks about,

Gets water from the well
whenever she is out.

Her pails are quite full;
she must surely be in pain,

But she smiles all the while
and she fills them up again.

I've never seen her rest
nor have you I surely doubt.

When knights jump on her buckets,
you never hear her shout.

When she passes by me kindly
I sing her a refrain,

But she smiles and walks right by me
to fill her pails again.

MOBILE GEAR

Name: Mobile Gear

Description: Ride over hazards and reach higher places! Hop on and hold on!

Location: Clockwork Tower

Price: ◊3,000 (Field); ◊3,500 (Village)

Magic Casting Cost: 6

Damage Points: 2

Tips and Tricks: Try using this relic against Tinker Knight to speed up the fight!

Ride Over Hazards and Reach Higher Places!

The Mobile Gear is one of the most unique relics that you'll ever see! It's gear with a platform for Shovel Knight to ride. It's great for getting ya around to secret spots, but it'll also take out some enemies along the way!

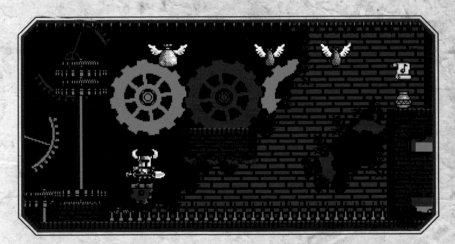

Ye Olde Relic Facts

❖ The Mobile Gear can be found in the Clockwork Tower, and it's a great way to get around that stage after you get it!

❖ Beat five enemies with one Mobile Gear to earn the Clearing a Path feat.

❖ The Mobile Gear can defeat the Tinker Knight in one hit.

WAR HORN

Name: War Horn

Description: Use a lot of magic to clear enemies around you with a powerful blow! A costly cacophony!

Location: Stranded Ship

Price: 🔹4,000 (Field); 🔹5,000 (Village)

Magic Casting Cost: 20

Damage Points: 5

Tips and Tricks: Try playing the War Horn for the Yoppler inside the Armor Outpost!

This is the War Horn! The most destruction-causing, enemy-beating relic you'll ever use! Just give it a blow and it'll destroy any enemy in your path!

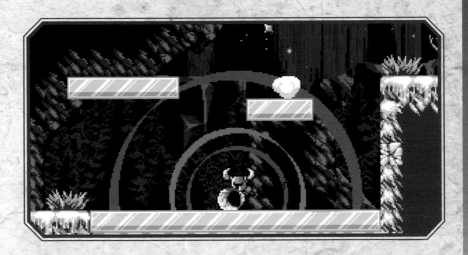

Ye Olde Relic Facts

❖ The War Horn is great for getting out of a tough spot, but it uses a lot of magic.

❖ Defeat 5 enemies with one blow of the War Horn to earn the Boom! feat!

Croaker Puns

Welcome back to Showtime at the Village Juice Bar! I'm Croaker and I'll be your host again tonight! Sorry I was late. I probably should have HOPPED a train!

I saw the Deer Lady the other day and we laughed and laughed. She's a lot of fawn.

Polar Knight's not such a bad guy! He can be a little cold, though.

The Bard has turned over a new leaf. It's true. He really changed his tune!

EXPERT HOOP ROLLING GUIDE WITH HOOP KID

Hiya, buddy! You ever played hoop rolling before?! Oh boy! It's the best game around! The rules are pretty tough, so lemme see if I can explain 'em right!

Step One: Roll the hoop!

Step Two: Bounce on the hoop!

Step Three: Keep bouncing, and make sure to stay over the hoop and avoid landing

Feat		
Hooper		Bounce on the Hoop Kid's hoop for five seconds.

That's it! I know it's a lot to take on all at once, but if you can get that down, you'll be a top hoop roller in no time! Be careful not to hit it too far away with a charge attack!

PROPELLER DAGGER

Name: Propeller Dagger

Description: Soar through the sky blade-first! Now you can reach all sorts of places!

Location: Flying Machine

Price: ⬦4,000 (Field); ⬦5,000 (Village)

Magic Casting Cost: 4

Damage Points: 1

Tips and Tricks: Use this relic to clear gaps you couldn't jump over before and to attack hard-to-reach enemies!

How do you make a knight fly? Give him a Propeller Dagger! Yeah, I know it wasn't funny. It wasn't supposed to be a joke! It's very serious stuff. With the Propeller Dagger you can fly through the air and get to new places that ya never could before!

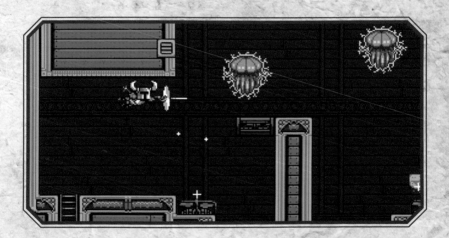

Ye Olde Relic Facts

- ❖ The Propeller Dagger can be found in the Flying Machine.

- ❖ Not only is it good for flying, it's great for combat!

- ❖ Defeat enough enemies while flying with the Propeller Dagger and you could earn the Flying feat!

FRIGID FLIGHT

The last of three Relic Courses.
You can only make it through
Frigid Flight by using the
Propeller Dagger relic!

Well, looks like that's it for the relics! I hope ya had a fun time learning about all the different magical items that your ol' pal Chester has for sale. May all of these relics bring you good fortune on your quest for SHOVEL JUSTICE! Bye!

Shovel Smith

If it's knowledge ye seek, ye've come to the right place, mate! The Shovel Smith ('at's me, by the way!) is the one to show ye all about the greatest weapon ever forged. Some say it's a sword, some say it's a shovel, but I'm here to tell ya, matie . . . it's the SHOVEL BLADE!

THE SHOVEL BLADE

The Shaft

Reinforced so ye can whack Tadvolts all day long without it bending.

The Handle

It's the part ye hold on to. Enhanced with a soft grip.

The Blade

Perfect for both slashing mercilessly
and digging tirelessly.

Feats completed with the Shovel Blade	
Sparker	Finish off any boss using the Ground Spark technique.
Master Shoveler	Purchase all available Shovel Blade upgrades.

SHOVEL BLADE UPGRADES

Shovel Blade Upgrade	Description
Charge Handle	Hold your attack to unleash a powerful charge slash!
Trench Blade	Dig up a whole pile in one mighty motion.
Drop Spark	Slash to spark the ground when you're at full health.

Greetings for the third time, traveler! You must know my name by now! After my last two ditties, I hope you're singing it from the rooftops! Well, I've got one more song for you! This one is called:

The Mighty Shovel Knight

He is the mighty Shovel Knight!

HOORAH!

HOORAH!

He'll fight the darkness! Bring the light!

HOORAH!

HOORAH!

He is the Mighty Shovel Knight!

He'll save us all and end this blight, the mighty Shovel Knight!

HOORAH!

HOORAHHHHH!!!

TROUPPLE ACOLYTE TEACHES YOU THE TROUPPLE KING DANCE

ALL HAIL THE TROUPPLE KING! And the best way to honor this courtly carp is to learn his dignified dance!

First, flap your fins!

Then, do a big stomp!

Now, turn left and right!

Like bomp bomp bomp bomp!

So, dance your dance!

With lots of noise!

Be louder than

All girls and boys!

Now, smile real big!

Then just one more thing!

Yell as loud as you can!

All hail the Troupple King!

Meet the Armorer

This be the Aerial Anvil! A forge high above Armor Outpost and the top spot in all the land to learn about armor! If you're THICK-SKINNED enough, that is! HAR HAR HAR! I'm just messin' with you, chum! You don't have to be so HARDHEADED about it! HAR HAR HAR!

STALWART PLATE

Your original armor. Simple, but sturdy.

Stalwart Plate is the original armor that we all know and love! It don't be as strong as the other armors I can make ya, but it's still as tough as nails! Plus, it comes in the best color of 'em all . . . SHOVEL KNIGHT CERULEAN BLUE! HAR HAR HAR!!

Armor Facts

- ❖ **Color:** Cerulean Blue
- ❖ **Armor Insights:** This is the armor that Shovel Knight starts his adventure wearing.
- ❖ **Cost:** 🔶0

FINAL GUARD

Drop half as much gold when you fall in battle!

Final Guard is a perfect set of armor for a miser! HAR HAR HAR! It's the cheapest armor yer gold can buy AND it helps you save money when yer slain in battle! I recommend this armor if yer a real PENNY-PINCHER! HAR HAR HAR!!

Armor Facts

- ❖ **Color:** Red
- ❖ **Armor Insights:** Great for any adventurer who needs a helping hand holding on to all their hard-earned riches!
- ❖ **Cost:** 3,000

CONJURER'S COAT

Sacrifice some protection for a higher magic limit, and harvest magic from defeated foes!

Conjurer's Coat is the best armor for all you spooky magic users! It increases your magic limit, turning you into one WIZ OF A WIZARD! HAR HAR HAR! All that power comes at a cost, though, chum! Conjurer's Coat decreases your defense, making you more vulnerable to enemy attacks! So choose, but choose wisely! Is this the armor for you?

Armor Facts

- ❖ **Color:** Purple
- ❖ **Armor Insights:** Only the most serious relic scholars should invest in an armor like this!
- ❖ **Cost:** 🪙 4,000

DYNAMO MAIL

Perform two consecutive Shovel Drops to unleash a powerful charge slash!

Repeat Shovel Drops down from the sky to charge up yer slash with the Dynamo Mail armor! Just as tough as Stalwart Plate but with 100 percent more charge-slashing action! Available now wherever armor is forged. So . . . right here! HAR HAR HAR!!

Armor Facts

- ❖ **Color:** Silver

- ❖ **Armor Insights:** Confident in your Shovel Drop combos? This may be the armor for you!

- ❖ **Cost:** 6,000

MAIL OF
MOMENTUM

Heavily plated. Keep your footing when struck by enemies, but stopping may be a problem!

Now we're gettin' to the good stuff, chum! If a bit more protection is what you require, ya can't do much better than the Mail of Momentum armor! It'll keep you from getting knocked back when yer hit, but be careful! Wearing armor as heavy as this also makes it tough to stop! We wouldn't want you falling in a pit or somethin', now would we?! HAR HAR HAR!!

Armor Facts

- ❖ **Color:** Black/Red
- ❖ **Armor Insights:** It may take some getting used to, but this armor is great for helping any adventurer stay grounded!
- ❖ **Cost:** 🪙6,000

ORNATE PLATE

Flashy! Acrobatic! Useless!

So ya like a bit of style over substance, do ya? Well then, Ornate Plate is probably the armor for you! It's basically good for nothin', but it do look pretty when it glints in the sun! HAR HAR HAR! You'll look like a real high roller when you've got this beauty on, and King Knight will definitely take notice of you!

Armor Facts

- ❖ **Color:** Gold

- ❖ **Armor Insights:** Flip with every jump, sparkle brightly with every step, and land on your feet when thrown from a catapult! This armor is strictly for showing off.

- ❖ **Cost:** ◍8,000

- ❖ Allows Shovel Knight to flip and jump gracefully.

SPECIAL ARMORS

Armor of Chaos (Sony)

A special red-and-white armor you can obtain after defeating Kratos. Once you get yer hands on this stuff, you'll be a God of War in no time!

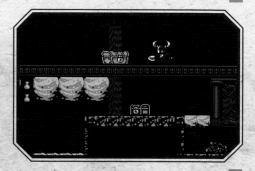

* ❖ Obtain the Grave Digger's Shovel and give it to the Armorer.

* ❖ When armor is equipped, Shovel Knight gains multiple hit combos.

* ❖ The Shovel Drop becomes sudden and immediate.

* ❖ If a red orb appears after defeating an enemy, Shovel Knight can use this to shoot a small wave of fire across the screen.

Farewell, my friend. It was nae enough time that we got to spend together. I wish we could talk 'bout Shovel Blades all day, but there is too much work to be done!

Toad Gear (Microsoft)

A rad set of armor you get from hangin' out with those cool bros, the Battletoads!

- ❖ Complete the Battletoads sidequest to obtain the gear.

- ❖ It can be equipped by talking to Zitz or visiting the Armorer or Goatarmorer.

- ❖ Shovel Knight can use this to attack and run faster, and end with a large combo hit.

- ❖ A power dive is also possible by pressing down in the air.

What was? Talking to me? That's weird—I thought we were friends. Come back around anytime if you want to talk about armor over a meal! I'll make you a plate! HAR HAR HAR!

I bid you good day and good luck in the fight ahead! Now that ya know all about the relics, weapons, and armor you can use on your quest, you have what it takes. Get out there—we are countin' on you to defeat the Order of No Quarter and the evil Enchantress!

Dictum summa! I am not a witch, but my third eye knows your useless infos!

You've read 79 pages with information about 11 relics 3 Shovel Blade upgrades and 8 armor sets

FEATS

Relic	Feats
Flare Wand Flare Wander	Defeat an enemy with the Flare Wand from more than twenty-five blocks away.
Propeller Dagger Flying Feat	Defeat three enemies using the Propeller Dagger without touching the ground.
Dust Knuckles Knuckle Down	Hang in the air for more than four seconds using the Dust Knuckles.
Fishing Rod Master Angler	Successfully fish five sparkling fishing spots.
Alchemy Coin Reflected Riches	Bounce the same Alchemy Coin five times in a row.
Mobile Gear Clearing a Path	Run over five enemies using the same Mobile Gear.
Phase Locket Another Dimension	Collect 2,000 worth of gold lying on spikes while using the Phase Locket.
Chaos Sphere Super Sphere	Destroy five enemies within five seconds using Chaos Spheres.
War Horn Boom!	Defeat five foes at once using the War Horn.
Throwing Anchor Arc of Iron	Defeat three enemies with one Throwing Anchor.
Trouple Chalice Trouple Acolyte	Discover the secrets of the Trouple King.